TERRARIUMS & KOKEDAMA

ALYSON MOWAT

Alyson Mowat founded her business in 2013 to create natural scenes and lush backdrops in urban settings. Prior to this, she moved from South Africa to London, where she trained as a graphic designer and worked in the fashion and jewellery industries. With a focus on hand-crafted, artisan pieces, Alyson draws on her passion for style and beautiful things when designing her collections. She also holds indoor planting workshops from her studio in London.

TERRARIUMS & KOKEDAMA

ALYSON MOWAT

**STYLISH IDEAS
FOR LOW-MAINTENANCE
INDOOR PLANTING**

PHOTOGRAPHY BY CATHERINE GRATWICKE

KYLE BOOKS

TO MY PARENTS,
JOAN AND PAUL MOWAT,
FOR MY ROOTS AND WINGS.

First published in Great Britain in 2017 by
Kyle Books, an imprint of Kyle Cathie Ltd
192–198 Vauxhall Bridge Road
London SW1V 1DX
general.enquiries@kylebooks.com
www.kylebooks.co.uk

10 9 8 7 6 5 4 3 2 1

ISBN 978 0 85783 437 9

Project Editor: Claire Rogers
Copy Editor: Jason Irving
Designer: Evi O. / OetomoNew
Photographer: Catherine Gratwicke
Illustrator: Christopher Moon
Prop Stylist: Nadine Tubbs
Stylist: Alyson Mowat
Production: Nic Jones, Gemma John and Lisa Pinnell

A Cataloguing in Publication record for this title is available
from the British Library.

Colour reproduction by ALTA London
Printed and bound in China by C&C
Offset Printing Co., Ltd.

CULTIVATE YOUR GREEN THUMB

CARING FOR YOUR HOUSEPLANTS

—

YOU HAD ME AT HAWORTHIA

For years prior to owning this particular succulent my interactions with plants were limited to the occasional visit to Kew. When I'd dabbled in plant ownership, it was without any real conviction or, more importantly, success. However, this chubby rosette of striped foliage was a revelation. It forgave my mistakes and even rewarded me with baby offsets when I was neglectful, which came as a big surprise. In return, I made it my mission to learn as much as possible about this scrappy underdog ... and the rest is history.

Many of my plant successes have grown from failure. Despite a few fatalities along the way, things started to look up when I fell in love with plants and persevered in trying to keep them alive. Like any relationship, the more you get to know a plant, the more invested you become; the more you discover, the more beguiling they appear. One night as you nod off, you'll find yourself trying to work out why your fern was looking a little weary today, only to wake up, excited, realising all it needed was a change of scenery, away from direct sunlight.

We need nature by our side. Plants look after us by purifying the air we breathe, reducing our stress levels, they even make us nicer people*.

I'm thrilled you are interested in creating plantscapes in your home. Here are some general potted houseplant tips, to clear up any grey areas.

---

*Ryan Richards and his team of researchers at the University of Rochester, in New York, proved that nature really does make us nicer, when they carried out experiments examining the effects of natural versus artificial environments.

1
WATER

Plants wilt when they are over-watered and they wilt when they are under-watered, so it can be hard to tell what's wrong. Overwatering is the surest way to kill a plant, causing root rot and a nasty pong, so use pots with drainage holes; no one wants to lie in a cold bath for weeks and roots need time to breathe and dry in between waterings. Since terrariums don't have drainage holes you need to be even more careful not to overwater them.

City water is not good for plants and can slow down growth. If you have the space, install a rain barrel and use the captured rainwater to water your plants. Alternatively, let tap water sit in a bucket for a couple of days to allow the chlorine to evaporate. Having water at room temperature is a good rule of thumb, as cold water can shock the system. If these options don't appeal, consider investing in a water purification system for your home, such as a reverse osmosis water filter.

To decide whether your pot plants need a drink, touch the soil. If it feels sticky and looks dark, skip on the watering. If the soil feels dry, water plants with confidence, ensuring the soil is soaked through. Use saucers under pots whenever possible and allow excess water to drain out of pots before placing them back on their saucers.

On average I water plants a couple of times a week in the summer and once a fortnight in the winter. Of course, each plant has different needs, so this is just a rough guide for plants in pots, not in terrariums (more about those later). It's tempting to stick to a schedule, but I'd advise observing your plants and feeling the soil instead.

2
LIGHT

Falling head over heels in love with a plant is easily done. It is tempting to purchase a plant based purely on its handsomeness, then proudly walk it home and position it in a spot that needs cheering. However, I recommend picking a plant based on your light levels. Contemplate the position you have in mind for a plant; is it sunny or shady? Direct sunlight can cause sunburn and singed leaves; most plants need bright but indirect light, so should be positioned a few feet away from a south-facing window. Do your homework, search online for 'plants that like a north-facing bathroom window', figure out which direction your windows face and what will thrive there, then make a shortlist of suitable plants. You can choose one from this list based on what you find most aesthetically pleasing.

3 FERTILISER

Fertiliser is a good idea, but if your main concern is simply keeping your plant alive don't get worked up about it. Fertiliser can transform your houseplant from weedy to wonderful, but too much will cause it to overdose and die.

If you decide to fertilise, it is best to do so in the warmer months when the plant is growing. Dilute fertilizer with water and administer in small doses. It is comparable to vitamin supplements. Plants are good at producing their own food but most will need a boost from time to time.

4 ROOM

If your plant's roots are circling and trying to escape through the drainage holes – take the hint! Roots should be within soil, not surrounding it; your plant has outgrown its home. Even without this telltale signal your plant will need to be repotted every year or two with spanking new soil for a nutrient boost. Try to do this in the spring.

5 HUMIDITY

Tropical plants, ferns, palms and orchids like it steamy and should be kept clear of heating contraptions that will dry them out. Adding pebbles and a little water to their saucer will boost humidity. They also enjoy a daily spritz from a mister. Do not mist cacti and succulents in between waterings … nothing will make them more homesick for the desert. Like all plants in your home, consider where they come from and aim to emulate their natural habitat.

6 NEGLECT

Know yourself and what sort of plant you want. There's one out there for everyone. Some plants can be needy. Others, like sansevieria (snake plant) or *Zamioculcas zamiifolia* (ZZ plant), are low maintenance. What's your schedule like? How often are you away? Research the plants beforehand, consider their profile … how compatible would you really be together in the long run?

—

'The power of Man over Nature is limited only by one condition, that it must be exercised in conformity with the laws of Nature.'
HERSCHEL

NATE FOREVER

HOW THE CLOSED TERRARIUM CAME ABOUT

—

Victorian London was a suffocating place. Polluted and grimy, it was not an obvious environment to indulge a passion for botany, but it was there, in the East End, that botanist Nathaniel Bagshaw Ward invented the Wardian case. The precursor to the terrarium as we know it today, its invention would dramatically change the future of botany and plant exploration.

In 1829, during a stroll in the Kent countryside, Nathaniel found the pupa of a Hawk moth. He placed the cocoon, along with its organic matter, into a hermetically sealed jar and took it home, then waited for the moth to pupate. To his surprise a fern sprouted from the organic matter and thrived in the jar, and the moth's meagre existence was forgotten. He had discovered that an uncontaminated atmosphere, moisture and appropriate light provided the ideal environment for plant growth.

This discovery was perfectly timed; the Victorians had a burgeoning interest in exotic plants and ferns. This obsession for ferns (pteridomania) invaded all aspects of life. As well as the living species being displayed in homes in Wardian cases, fern motifs and designs were commonplace on carpets, curtains and wallpaper. Even custard cream biscuits couldn't escape being stamped with the design of a fern's fronds.

The good doctor's invention also allowed explorers to safely transport plants from their expeditions back to England. Wardian cases protected them from salt water and rodents, keeping them sealed and contained in their own biosphere.

Eventually Wardian cases fell out of favour, but in the 1960s and 1970s growing plants under glass became fashionable again with the creation of the bottle garden, which required the skill of wiggling plants through thin bottlenecks and the patience of a saint – or myriad bamboo tools and DIY planting devices (see page 14).

The terrarium remains a beautiful way of bringing the outdoors inside, providing the conditions essential for a moisture-loving tropical garden to flourish within our dry, centrally heated homes.

PROJECT

1

TOOLS
MONEY
CAN'T
BUY

TOOLS MONEY CAN'T BUY

THE TERRARIUM TOOLKIT

—

In some of the terrariums you attempt to fill, keeping calm whilst trying to squeeze a niggly plant through a tight opening will seem near impossible. Stress levels begin to soar and what should be a moment of serenity and reconnection with nature may instead make you want to throw the whole maddening thing in the bin.

Overcome such trials and tribulations with a little preparation and a DIY terrarium toolkit, fit for a green-fingered demigod.

For the projects in this book, you will need a range of tools, including:

- Long chefs' tweezers / Chopsticks (The Picker-Upper)
- Straws (The Dirt Blower)
- Card / paper funnel (The Dropper-Inner)
- Baster / Pipette (The Water-Squirter)
- Scissors / aquarium plant scissors
- Bamboo stick tools (see opposite)

YOU WILL NEED

HOLLOW BAMBOO, CUT INTO 30CM LENGTHS
You can usually purchase these pre-cut at your local flower market or garden centre. You will need one piece per tool.

CRAFT KNIFE

TWINE / WIRE

PLIERS

SUPERGLUE (FOR THE SOIL COMPRESSOR)

For the bamboo stick tools

STEEL SPOON (THE DIGGER)

STEEL FORK (THE RAKER AND MOSS-FLUFFER)

PAINTBRUSH (THE CLEANER-UPPER)

BLADE (THE PRUNER)

BORED CORK OR RUBBER BUNG (THE SOIL COMPRESSOR)

SPONGE / KITCHEN PAPER (THE CLEANER)

METHOD

1   Slide one tool into each length of bamboo until it feels secure. Often spoons, forks, paintbrushes and blades will slide straight in, however you may need to split the bamboo if you need a bit of extra give. To do this, take a small craft knife and cut a cross into the end of the tip … There, it should fit better now. For The Cleaner, attach the sponge to the end of a bamboo stick and wrap to secure it using wire.

2   To keep the tools in place, wrap twine tightly around the bamboo surrounding each tool and tie a knot. Ensure you are forceful with your wrapping. Is the tool secure within the bamboo? There is nothing worse than losing your spoon to the dark depths of a terrarium, then having to create another tool to fish it out.

3   Use pliers to bend fork tines and the spoon bowl to create a rake and spade. As you start using your tools you may want to adjust them to suit your requirements.

4   To make 'The Soil Compressor', squeeze a piece of bamboo into the hole of the cork or rubber bung, so that there's no give. A couple of drops of superglue around the hole should keep it securely in place.

5   Watch your collection of bespoke tools expand over time … and you'll have whatever you need to access the far-flung corners of your terrarium.

IT'S
LIKE
A SAUNA
IN HERE

IT'S LIKE
A SAUNA IN HERE

TROPICAL / CLOSED TERRARIUM

—

INSIDE A CLOSED TERRARIUM, I.E. A GLASS VESSEL WITH A LID

As the temperature within the terrarium rises during the day, moisture from the soil and plants evaporates, condensing as droplets on the inside of the glass, then trickling down the side of the vessel back into the soil. Plants use water, carbon dioxide and light to produce oxygen and sugar through photosynthesis. At night the opposite occurs, with the plant using oxygen and producing carbon dioxide. In a terrarium, plants continuously recycle the carbon dioxide and oxygen they need to survive.

YOU WILL NEED

TERRARIUM TOOLKIT (PAGE 17)

GLASS VESSEL
(e.g. apothecary bottle, carboy – brewers use these to make wine or beer,
clip-top jar with rubber seal removed, jam jar... pretty much any glass vessel
that has a lid or makeshift equivalent)

SLATE, PEBBLES OR GRAVEL

HORTICULTURAL OR ACTIVATED CHARCOAL

POTTING SOIL
(organic, if possible, with no added fertiliser or crawling interlopers)

TROPICAL PLANTS
such as tropical ferns (*Peperomia spp.*), earth stars (*Cryptanthus spp.*),
begonias (*Begonia spp.*), African violets (*Saintpaulia spp.*), nerve plants
(*Fittonia spp.*), creeping fig (*Ficus pumila*), baby's tears (*Soleirolia soleirolii*),
polka dot plant (*Hypoestes phyllostachya*). Garden centres are starting to
cater better for miniature gardens.

BUN MOSS
also called cushion moss (*Leucobryum spp.*)
(this is the verdant jewel in the crown, but all moss is worthy of your love)

OPTIONAL
quartz, fossils, old wasp nests, shells, animal skulls (although be wary of mould).
Add your own DIY clay mushrooms – see Project 11 (page 76).

METHOD

1 Select your glass vessel – I would always suggest using clear glass, but if your vessel has a slight tint to it, move it closer to the light source than you usually would once planted – give it a good clean and let it dry out.

2 Wearing gloves (if you want to; you may, like me, enjoy getting your hands dirty), tilt the vessel on its side and gently add a few centimetres of slate or pebbles, one stone at a time, to avoid breaking the glass. This is the drainage layer and helps to ensure excess water doesn't stay in the soil and cause root rot. Since we are working in an enclosed space, the crucial drainage layer prevents the terrarium from turning into a glass-encased swamp; who would want that?

3 Add around a tablespoon of activated charcoal, or more if you are working in a larger vessel. In a closed environment, charcoal helps to remove odour and toxins associated with standing water, keeping the soil 'sweet'. As water passes through the charcoal, impurities are trapped so the water is cleaner for the next cycle. Activated charcoal is used in aquarium filters and can be purchased in most aquatic or pet stores.

4 Grab handfuls of soil and add through a funnel or, if you can reach inside, place on top of the drainage and charcoal layers. The amount of soil you include will vary according to the size of your vessel, however the soil line should rest just below the halfway mark. Lightly pat down with your fingers or the bored cork tool (without compressing the soil too much), lowering the soil level down further.

5 Burrow into the soil using circular motions (the other 'unattached to a tool' side of your bamboo stick is a worthy tunnel-maker).

6 Arrange the plants outside your glass vessel; moving pots around to find the perfect pose. Once you find the arrangement you like, remove the largest plant from its pot first. Dust off soil from plant roots.

7 Lower plant down using tongs or chopsticks and nestle roots neatly into holes. You can also wrap leafy plants in a paper cylinder, making it easier to slip them through narrow bottlenecks.

8 Continue planting, ensuring plants have enough room to breathe and are not pressed up against the glass.

9 Press soil firmly around roots using the cork tool. Add clumps of moss. Press the green side against the inside of the glass as you slide it down. Gently manoeuvre the moss underneath the leaves until you have a carpet of moss covering sections of soil. Avoid showing off the brown bits or rhizoids underneath. If the moss is too dry it will flake off the main clump and look unsightly.

10 Accessorise with objects such as quartz and fossils that visually enhance your terrarium, or add items that you have an affinity with.

11 Dust leaves with the paintbrush tool or blow off dirt with a straw. Use The Cleaner tool (see page 17) to wipe down the glass walls inside your terrarium. Lightly administer water using a baster or pipette to settle plants in, before sealing the terrarium shut.

CARE

WATER

Overwatering is one of the most common mistakes; the worst thing you can do in
a terrarium is to overwhelm plants with water. If looking a little sludgy, remove the
terrarium's lid for a couple of days to let it dry out a bit. Water droplets forming on the
glass is a good sign; it means things are chugging along nicely. During the day, you
want to see around 50 per cent condensation on the glass of your tropical terrariums,
the rest of the glass should be clear.

PLACE IN INDIRECT LIGHT

Direct light can act like a magnifying glass and fry a terrarium's contents, turning the
lushest jungle-in-a-jar into a brittle crisp. If light only reaches the terrarium from one
side, you should rotate the terrarium every couple of days to ensure the plants don't all
grow at an angle pointing towards the light. Rotating the terrarium will force the plants
to grow tall and straight. Every fortnight or so, take the lid off your terrarium and allow
it to breathe for a few hours.

LOW, BUT NOT NO, MAINTENANCE

To prevent plants outgrowing the terrarium and sneaking up on you, reach inside and
trim. Use aquarium plant scissors if you can't get a regular pair through the opening.

When flowers pass on, you'll want to remove their heads and any leaves that are
brown or have fallen with chopsticks.

Mould has got to go! The slightest hint of the stuff and I'm in there with a magnifying
glass. The first thing to try is removing the lid for a few days; if this doesn't rectify the
problem, remove the mould or the affected plant entirely (your long chefs' tweezers will
come in handy here). If you notice mould forming on the surface, improve soil drainage
with your bamboo fork tool, by mixing it up a little.

Doing the windows and a bit of housekeeping from time to time will keep plants and
their admirers in high spirits.

Cacti and succulents will not appreciate you putting a lid on it. They prefer to feel the
dry fresh air between their leaves and spikes. So be patient, we'll be using some of
these plants in later projects. Can't wait!

PROJECT
3

THE
LIFE
SCIENTIFIC

THE LIFE SCIENTIFIC

CONICAL FLASK TERRARIUM

—

Who said algae was nothing more than pond scum? Someone who'd never encountered marimo algae, obviously. These fuzzy balls of love prove that what the world has been missing all along is plant Furbies!

Japanese folklore tells the tale of two young sweethearts whose forbidden love affair resulted in them running away together. In the end a watery death befell the star-crossed lovers when they drowned in Lake Akan, however, their hearts metamorphosed into little marimo balls that tumbled along together, living happily ever after.

Marimo ('ball seaweed' in Japanese) is known as the 'love plant'. The balls are considered good-luck charms for those looking for love, those hoping to mend a relationship and those looking to heal a broken heart. Red roses? Blah … marimo balls make for unique love tokens.

These low-maintenance, downy spheres look striking when simply displayed. I like to keep my marimo minimal, teaming them with a little sand or pebbles. Add drama by including a sea fan or shells to the conical flask.

YOU WILL NEED

CONICAL FLASK, ALSO KNOWN AS
AN ERLENMEYER FLASK
Any jar will do here. I just happen to think
marimo look rather fetching bopping around
in lab equipment.

TERRARIUM TOOLKIT

SAND OR SMALL PEBBLES

OPTIONAL
shells, sea fan, wood – ensure your added extras fit
through your vessel's opening

MARIMO BALL
Spherical growth of *Aegagropila linnaei* –
available from aquarium shops

METHOD

1   Rinse out your flask, avoiding detergents and soap.

2   Create a funnel from paper and add around
    5cm of sand or stones.

3   Add other elements, if you so wish, anchoring the
    sea fan or wood into the sand or small pebbles
    with your chopsticks.

4   Top up the flask with room-temperature water.
    For best results, allow water to sit for a couple
    of days before adding it to your flask for the
    first time and when changing the water every
    fortnight.

5   Now for the pièce de résistance; add marimo!

CARE

Marimo balls are not high maintenance and can live for over 100 years. Now that's long-lasting love.

WATER
Change fortnightly, although water will evaporate more in the summer so switch to weekly water changes over the warmer months.

LIGHT
Place in low to medium indirect light. If marimo start to look a little brown, come away from the light … it's too hot!

—

TIP

FOR A FULLER-FIGURED MARIMO
Emphasise marimo's curvaceous assets; these may flatten out over time, settling on the floor of your aquatic scene. Keep marimo in shape by stirring the water occasionally with a chopstick, rousing them from the bottom and nudging them gently, so that they rest on a different side than they had previously. This simple action mimics the currents of their natural habitats.

PROJECT

4

TIP #1:
'ALWAYS LOOK
FABULOUS DARLING!'

TIP #1:
'ALWAYS LOOK FABULOUS DARLING!'

TIPS FOR GROWING ORCHIDS BEHIND GLASS

—

ABOUT

The Orchidaceae are widely spread over both hemispheres and are made up of over 25,000 wild species, making the orchid family one of the largest. There are two main types: epiphytic (growing on trees) and terrestrial (growing in the ground).

There are a couple of different options for growing orchids behind glass, depending on the needs of your plant. Always attempt to replicate the plant's natural habitat by researching it in advance. Intimately getting to know their habits and quirks will help you to understand what makes them tick and you'll reap the most rewards in the long run.

NATURE'S MOST OUTRAGEOUS FLIRT AND GREATEST TRICKSTER

Nothing says 'crazy stupid love' like orchids. Personality doesn't really come into it for orchids; they've come to rely upon their looks and perfume. Some will flirt outrageously, luring in their pollinator by disguising themselves as an object of desire. A naïve, usually young male, insect advances on an orchid who is masquerading as a beautiful lady insect. She may actually be interested in him, as she's not buzzing off in the opposite direction. He fumbles a little as he attempts to unsuccessfully mate with her, picking up a clump of pollen grains on his back rather than a notch on his bedpost. It's all a bit cringeworthy, really, but he finally moves on only to be tempted by another pseudo mate who he then transfers the pollen to.

EPIPHYTIC ORCHID TERRARIUM

—

Epiphytic orchids anchor themselves onto other plants. They have thick roots covered with silvery valamen, this protects the roots and acts like a sponge, collecting water and nutrients. Because they grow with their roots out of the ground, covering them up and compacting them with soil is a terrible idea, so here we give them some air. Epiphytic orchids include moth orchids (*Phalaenopsis spp.*), *Masdevallia spp.*, *Cattleya spp.*, *Dendrobium spp.*, *Oncidium spp.*

YOU WILL NEED

TALL GLASS VESSEL WITH OR WITHOUT A LID

STONES OR PEBBLES

PURIFIED WATER

A LARGE NAIL OR AWL

PLIERS

A LIT CANDLE TO HEAT UP THE NAIL OR AWL

A CLEAR PLASTIC POT
(a similar size or slightly bigger than the pot your orchid was purchased in)

ORCHID BARK

BUCKET

ACTIVATED CHARCOAL

PERLITE (OPTIONAL)

EPIPHYTIC ORCHID (NOTHING TOO BIG)

DRIFTWOOD OR MOSS, TO LOOSELY COVER AND DECORATE AROUND THE POT

METHOD

The glass vessel

1   Give the glass vessel a really good clean before planting. Add about 5cm of small stones or pebbles to the bottom of your glass vessel.

2   Fill with 2cm of purified water to increase the humidity in the vessel (of course, orchids like it steamy). The water should not reach the bottom of the orchid pot.

The clear plastic pot

3   Open windows as burning plastic fumes are smelly. Grip the nail or awl with pliers and hold the point over a flame.

4   Push the hot nail into the side of the plastic pot; avoid fingers and avoid pushing all the way through to the opposite side of the plastic.

5   Repeat, punching holes in vertical lines throughout the plastic pot. Don't forget a few at the bottom, too. This is to allow for as much air to pass through the roots as possible in the still terrarium environment.

Orchid

6   Place enough bark in a bucket to fill your clear plastic pot and mix in a tablespoon of activated charcoal. Add a little perlite, if you wish, for a faster-draining mix.

7   Gently remove your orchid from its pot, shake off and throw away the old potting medium. Snip away mouldy, hollow roots up to the lighter healthier-looking section of roots.

8   Add a handful of the bark, charcoal and perlite (optional) mix to around the halfway mark of the plastic pot.

9   Now add the orchid, then the orchid mix, filling in the pot. Leave out the roots that seem happy to hang out over the pot.

10   Place the pot on top of the stones in the glass vessel and surround loosely with pieces of driftwood or moss to disguise the plastic pot. Voilà, it's a work of 'plart' (plant art)!

CARE

WATER
Once a week remove the orchid, in its plastic pot, from the glass vessel and saturate with rain or purified water over a sink. This will push air and built-up minerals through the roots. Mist leaves and aerial roots throughout the week.

Orchids love high air humidity but hate having wet feet, which causes roots to become soft and soggy. When you top up the water in your terrarium's drainage layer, ensure that it does not reach the plastic pot.

Whoever started the rumour about watering orchids with ice cubes has been vilified enough by orchid lovers all over the world. Repeat after me … 'not a good idea'. Save ice cubes for your gin and tonic instead.

Don't water orchids from above into leaves. Water left between leaves can cause crown rot, which is a major killer of orchids.

LIGHT
Bright, indirect light; think dappled.

AIR
I recommend removing the lid of your terrarium, if it has one, every couple of days for a few hours to allow for an airing.

FERTILISER
Your orchid will need to be fed, but not too much. Use a weak solution of orchid plant food when you water, i.e. 'weakly weekly'. Overfeeding will cause them to burn out.

NEGLECT
When your orchid has lost its flower, the plant is not dead. It's saving itself for its next divine bloom. Make a clean cut between the lowest withered bloom on the stem and the node (small bump) just below it. Rub a little cinnamon powder on the cut to help heal it. Bear with your orchid; it needs its rest and downtime just like you do.

TERRESTRIAL ORCHIDS

—

It was tempting to stick to epiphytes with this project as most of the orchids commonly available fall into this category, however, it means leaving out these absolute *dahlings*: the jewel orchid (*Ludisia discolor*) and slipper orchid (*Paphiopedilum*), and I honestly don't think I could sleep at night without at least offering an introduction.

Jewel orchids are coveted for their foliage rather than their flowers. Gold threads appear to be woven through some leaves while others are burgundy with a sumptuous velvety feel. Jewel orchids flower every winter; their delicate white flowers have a subtle but delicious citrusy fragrance.

To plant terrestrial orchids like the Jewel orchid see Project 2 Tropical Terrariums, and use an African violet mix instead of regular potting soil. Another tip is to make your drainage layer a little thicker than usual. If you are planting a semi-terrestrial slipper orchid, add a few pieces of bark into the soil around the roots.

Other terrestrial orchids include the nun orchid (*Phaius tancarvilleae*), bamboo orchid (*Arundina graminifolia*) and Brassia, the spider orchid (*Caladenia spp.*). Care for your earthbound orchid as you would the other plants in a tropical terrarium.

If you would like to add other plants to your terrestrial orchid terrarium consider African violets (*Saintpaulia spp.*), begonias (*Begonia spp.*) and soft mounds of bun moss (*Leucobryum spp.*).

—

INTERESTING FACT

Victorian women were not allowed to grow orchids, as they were dogged by erotic interpretations and deemed improper by polite society at the time. There can be no escaping the yonic portrayal and associations with orchid flowers, particularly in the work of Georgia O'Keeffe, which sent pulses racing in the 1920s.

THEIR BARK
IS WORSE THAN
THEIR BITE ...
UNLESS YOU'RE A FLY

THEIR BARK
IS WORSE THAN THEIR BITE...
UNLESS YOU'RE A FLY

CARNIVOROUS BOG TERRARIUM

—

THE FEMME FATALE

Whilst orchids use their wiles to lure insects in, dusting themselves with pollen to be carried on to the next flower, there have been no known cases of an orchid ever resorting to violence. There is one classification of plant however, with a much darker allure – carnivorous plants (CPs). From flies to rats, these femme fatales of the plant world ensnare and restrain unsuspecting victims, gradually turning their insides into a nutritional smoothie.

CPs include Venus fly traps, pitcher plants, butterworts, bladderworts, nepenthes, cobra lilies and sundews.

MAKING THE CASE

I like to house my potted CPs in an open Wardian case, but feel free to cover them with any glass or clear plastic contraption, preferably one with a few holes or an opening otherwise it can become too stuffy.

I prefer to grow CPs in different pots with saucers; they will be happy under the same glass roof but have different growing requirements that we need to acknowledge. It's also easy to clean the case and remove plants requiring a winter dormancy period.

MOST CARNIVOROUS PLANTS FALL INTO THE FOLLOWING TWO CATEGORIES:

Temperate CPs require a dormant season of a few months over winter. Their foliage will die back and they'll appreciate a cool dark room out of their case. Eye masks are optional, but rest is essential, as these temptresses need their beauty sleep.

Tropical CPs don't require a period of dormancy. They can stay warm in the case whilst temperate CPs are taking some time out from their busy and murderous schedule.

THE USUAL SUSPECTS

Trumpet pitcher (*Sarracenia spp.*) is an exceptional beauty boasting the most impressive foliage. These relatively easy growers will require a dormant period.

The Venus fly trap (*Dionaea muscipula*) does not like to be teased, excessively springing the trap will eventually kill Venus; make offerings of small insects instead. They require a dormant period.

The cobra lily (*Darlingtonia californica*) has a globular head, a forked foliage tongue and could not look any more lethal if it tried. Cobra lilies need their rest and a dormant period.

Butterworts (*Pinguicula spp.*) have leaves like sticky flypaper; you wouldn't want to put a foot wrong if you were an inquisitive insect. No dormancy needed.

*Sundews (*Drosera spp.*) are similar to butterworts. Creepy-crawlies get stuck on leaves and are digested. Unlike temperate sundews, tropical sundews do not require a dormant period.

Bladderworts (*Utricularia spp.*) I have a real soft spot for these pretties. They have hidden bladder-like structures beneath the surface, preferring to do their killing under a cloak of soil. Most of them don't require a dormant period.

Tropical pitcher plants (*Nepenthes spp.*) commonly called monkey cups, they like to keep their cups half full with water. Creatures unable to escape the cup's slippery slope eventually drown, before being digested. As they are tropical, no dormancy is required.

Australian pitcher plant (*Cephalotus follicularis*) chubby little cephs reminiscent of yawning toads … utterly adorable and highly desired by CP lovers. No dormancy required.

—

'I care more about Drosera*
than the origin of all the species in the world.'
CHARLES DARWIN

FOUND AT THE CRIME SCENE

GLOVES

SPHAGNUM PEAT MOSS*

COARSE HORTICULTURAL SAND OR PERLITE

BUCKET

GLAZED CERAMIC POTS WITH DRAINAGE HOLES AND SAUCERS
Your pots should be slightly bigger than the ones your carnivorous plants were purchased in
(if they came in pots). Keep the pot size in proportion to the plant.

SPHAGNUM MOSS (*SPHAGNUM SPP.*)

RAINWATER

A SELECTION OF PLANTS FROM 'THE IDENTITY PARADE'

GLASS CASE LARGE ENOUGH TO HOUSE YOUR CPS,
PREFERABLY WITH AN OPENING WINDOW

*In an attempt to cut down on my peat consumption I've been experimenting with organic coir and perlite. At the moment, it is too early to say how successful this has been, but I share the opinion of many that we need to find sustainable and effective alternatives to this wonderful resource. When using peat, use it wisely.

METHOD

1 Put on your gloves and prepare the soil for your CPs. Each species prefers its own particular soil blend, but for a general mix that works for most carnivorous plants, mix together 50 per cent peat moss and 50 per cent horticultural sand or perlite in a bucket. Sand and perlite should be rinsed a few times with rain or purified water.

2 Line the base of each pot, covering holes, with sphagnum moss. Add the soil mix, filling your pots halfway before tamping down with your fingers.

3 Water the potted soil with rainwater.

4 Overturn a pot containing a plant, holding the plant and soil as they slide out. The aim is to be non invasive to the roots and keep as much of this potting medium as possible.

5 Plant in the new pot. Add more of the soil blend around the clump surrounding the root ball. Secure roots by pushing down soil around them. Ensure your roots are buried deep when planting and the green crown of the plant is above the soil.

6 Give your newly potted plant a drink, and wash away any mud that has stuck to foliage. Place the pot on a saucer or tray and add to the glass case.

7 Repeat steps 4–6 for your remaining plants. Hanging plants will need to be lifted off the base.

CARE

NOT GUILTY ... A GAL'S GOTTA EAT, TOO!

It's amusing to imagine CPs plotting their next victim's downfall, but their carnivorousness actually developed to overcome harsh conditions. They have grown up in soil lacking nutrients and evolved to derive minerals from the critters they consume. Murderous tendencies aside, these plants are the fighting heroes of nature's struggle to survive.

BURN OUT

I really cannot stress enough how important it is to strip away all nutrients and minerals found in soil and water when growing CPs. As with most plants, always consider their natural environment and try to replicate this as closely as possible.

VENTILATION

Avoid a hermetically sealed vessel. A gap or opening will help keep mould at bay and provide adequate air circulation.

SUNLIGHT

CPs do appreciate high levels of light. I would recommend grow-lights if you intend to take this relationship to the next level or if your part of the world is as grey as mine. Avoid light during a temperate CP's dormancy.

WATER

Mist in the morning and evening with purified water to increase humidity and air movement. Pure water is essential, so only use water free from minerals (usually salts). Use rainwater or invest in a reverse osmosis system for your home if you plan to get serious with your CPs.

Unlike with regular potted plants, you should top up saucers or trays, ensuring they are always filled with water. I generally preach that less is more when it comes to watering, but these carnivores are an over-waterer's dream come true.

WINTER DORMANCY PERIOD FOR TEMPERATE CPS

Remove temperate plant pots individually and place them in an unheated shed, conservatory or garage. Like some animals, temperate perennials have adapted to cold winters and need to hibernate. All activity is reduced to a minimum as they recharge their batteries. If you skip the dormancy period your plant will become overworked and die of exhaustion within a few years. Cut down on watering (leaving the soil only slightly damp), feeding and turn off the lights. Tropical CPs can stay put, cosy and fed, inside the warm case all year round.

FEEDING

If the thought of lavishing your CPs with a spread of dried or live insects makes you feel woozy, fear not. I feed mine with betta fish pellets. The CPs don't seem to mind and every now and again, to keep them in the game, I'll throw in a dead fly recovered from a dusty windowsill.

PROJECT
6

AN
OASIS
IN THE
DESERT

AN OASIS IN THE DESERT

INDOOR SUCCULENT GARDEN

—

Create an oasis of calm and tranquillity, within an arid landscape of desert sand. Succulents and cacti make for relaxed, undemanding companions. A unique beauty lies in their quirky character and unusual form; some varieties look like they are visiting from another planet, with sci-fi-style foliage and flowers that explode with colour, boasting their own seasonal fireworks display.

These Suckers and Cool Cacts store their own water supply in fleshy leaves and swollen stems. They are perfectly suited to an open vessel and won't stand for the over-the-top moisture levels found in a closed terrarium.

YOU WILL NEED

TERRARIUM TOOLKIT (PAGE 17)

OPEN GLASS VESSEL

SLATE, PEBBLES OR GRAVEL

CARD

SCISSORS

TAPE

ACTIVATED CHARCOAL

CACTUS / SUCCULENT SOIL MIX
Blend your own by mixing 50 per cent regular potting soil with 50 per cent horticultural sand or grit. This makes for a fast-draining mixture that retains little moisture.

SELECTION OF PLANTS
Include cacti (Cactaceae family) and succulents such as aloes (*Aloe spp.*), echeverias (*Echeveria spp.*), living stones (*Lithops spp.*) and sedums (*Sedum spp.*)

LEATHER OR HEAVY-DUTY GARDENING GLOVES
(cactus spikes are nippy and a pain to remove)

SELECTION OF DIFFERENT EARTHY TONED SANDS
WITH A SIMILAR GRAIN SIZE

SKEWER OR KNITTING NEEDLE (OPTIONAL)

DECORATIVE ELEMENTS SUCH AS CRYSTALS

METHOD

1 Fill your glass vessel with a few centimetres of slate, pebbles or gravel for drainage.

2 Create an inner border of card with a smaller circumference than the glass vessel. Attach card ends with a little tape. The card should be a couple of centimetres away from the glass throughout, giving you a separate outer cavity to eventually build up the layers of coloured sand.

3 Sprinkle a tablespoon of activated charcoal within the card wall.

4 Fill with soil mix to whatever height you want your plants to perch, still working within the inner wall.

5 Before you start planting, think carefully about the design. Shuffle the plants around while they are still in their plastic pots, as you may wish to experiment with composition.

6 Using a bamboo stick, burrow holes in the soil, large enough to nest in succulent and cacti roots.

7 When un-potting plants wear gloves, and remove with care. Watch out for those nasty cacti pricks. Start planting, tamping down the soil around roots. You can ensure the plant is secure by giving it a gentle tug. Once the plants are in, dust them off gently with your bamboo paintbrush tool.

8 Now start to pour your first colour of sand between the card and the side of the glass. You can create a funnel from paper to help direct the flow of sand. Layer on another colour, paying attention to the patterns you are starting to create. A skewer or knitting needle is a great tool to help create different patterns in your sand. Use the sharp tip to push one colour into another. I like to replicate the earthy tones of rock strata when creating my layers, however, don't be afraid to experiment with more brightly coloured shades, too. Keep adding sand, experimenting with different layer thicknesses. Stop pouring when the sand is close to reaching the top edge of the card, reserving your final colour to cover the soil.

9 Now very gently raise the card out of the vessel, lifting evenly with both hands. Take your time, as you do not want to disturb the layers too much. Select your final colour and spread across the entirety of the surface, covering the soil as well as the built-up layers of sand.

10 Add finishing touches. Chunks of desert rose and peachy cerussite crystals complement the colour palette of the plants and the desert. Step back and admire your creation.

LET THERE BE LIGHT
Succulents stretch upwards when they aren't getting enough sunlight. Help a Sucker out and move them into a brighter spot.

NOT BIG DRINKERS
Treat 'em mean and keep 'em keen. You can usually revive a parched succulent, but there is no coming back from overwatering succulents and cacti in a vessel with no drainage holes. Allow for the soil to dry out in between watering Add water with a pipette as close to the base of the plant as possible. Reduce watering to a minimum over autumn and winter, this will encourage plants to rest.

KEEPING IT FRESH IN THE BEDROOM
At night, most plants consume and compete with us for oxygen. Succulents, however, use a different type of photosynthesis called CAM (Crassulacean acid metabolism), where the stomata in their leaves open at night, allowing them to collect carbon dioxide rather than release it.

PROJECT

7

THE
LIFE
AQUATIC
JARRARIUMS

THE LIFE
AQUATIC JARRARIUMS

PLANT YOUR OWN AQUATIC LANDSCAPE IN A JAR

—

Jarrariums are little self-contained ecosystems where aquatic plants are grown indoors in glass vessels. It took me a while to get round to plunging into the watery depths because assembling one felt a bit upside down to begin with. I also had to contend with the childhood memory of the frogspawn I'd collected and treasured in a jar. A much-younger me had hoped for a frog family of my own, but never quite made it past the stagnant-soup stage. Once I got the hang of a jarrarium, however, there was so much joy to be found.

Discover a whole new world of plants you never knew existed, how to layer aquatic greens (creating submerged and floating landscapes) and the oh-so-soothing effect of watching plants dance gracefully underwater, which somehow flicks a switch in our sensory overloaded brains.

Aquatic plants are forgotten members of the plant world, which is a pity as they're often very well suited for indoor growing. They have adapted to live completely submerged in water or drifting freely, without a care in the world, on the water's surface. I use a cylindrical glass vessel to demonstrate, however, you can find a piece of glassware that works best for you.

After experimenting with different techniques my favourite system for growing aquatic plants is the most natural and simplest. It is known as 'The Walstad Method' and was made popular by Diana Walstad. If you're interested in learning more, I recommend her book *Ecology of the Planted Aquarium*.

YOU WILL NEED

BUCKETS (FOR SOIL, PEBBLES AND WATER)

AQUATIC POND SOIL OR REGULAR POTTING SOIL,
ideally without the addition of chemical fertilisers
or perlite

SMALL PEBBLES

GLASS VESSEL

TERRARIUM TOOLKIT (PAGE 17)

AQUATIC PLANTS
Aquarium suppliers and speciality nurseries
sell a variety of suitable plants. I frequently
include the following plants in my jarrariums:
water hyacinth (*Eichhornia crassipes*)*, water sprite
(*Ceratopteris thalictroides*), amazon sword
(*Echinodorus amazonicus*), balansae plant
(*Cryptocoryne balansae*), *ludwigia peruensis*
(*Ludwigia glandulosa*), crimson ivy (*Hemiographis
colorata*), java fern (*Microsorum pteropus*),
Alternanthera cardinalis, *Hemiographis silverqueen*

FUNNEL (OPTIONAL)

HOSE (OPTIONAL)

METHOD

1   Fill a bucket one quarter full of soil and top up
with water. Clean the soil by swirling around
the mud at the bottom of the bucket, then leave
the muddy mush to sit still for a couple of hours.
Pieces of bark and debris should start to creep
towards the surface.

2   Place the small pebbles in a separate bucket
and follow the same procedure. Give the pebbles
a really good spin; the water should become
cloudy with pebble dust. Empty the water from
the bucket, refill with clean water, then repeat.
The aim is to get the water as clear as possible.

3   Fill a few buckets with water and let them reach
room temperature. These will fill the jarrarium.

4   Give your glass vessel a good rinse and wipe
clean. Don't use soap or detergent, as this will
affect the underwater environment and make it
difficult for plants to breathe. All this cleaning is
tiring work. Go and make yourself a cuppa and
contemplate the impossibility of what you are
trying to do … who on earth cleans soil?!

5   Return to your bucket of mud, remove the larger
pieces of debris and pour out the water, keeping
the heavier stuff at the bottom.

6   Now for the fun: Take around 3cm of the washed
soil, squeezing out the moisture before placing
it into your vessel. Avoid the temptation to make
mud pies instead. Separate the plants that need
to be rooted in soil from those that will float.
Floating plants are added last.

---

*Water hyacinths are invasive; so don't introduce them into a pond.

7   Remove plants from their pots and rinse the roots to remove any potting mix. Give the entire plant a good soak. You may need to trim down the root volume, as the soil in the glass vessel is shallow.

8   Get planting; the more the merrier, as plants will help to out-compete algae for nutrients. Add a few centimetres of pebbles on top of the mud, anchoring in the plants using your terrarium tools to help you.

9   Add water tentatively so as not to disturb the soil. I usually enlist another pair of hands here as I pour the buckets of room-temperature water through a funnel and hose. Use the side of the vessel or something flattish or spatula-like to block the main force of the water. Your first lot of water will probably look cloudy, so keep adding water, allowing your jarrarium to flood over until the water starts to look clear.

10 Now add your floating plants. Ah bliss, give your underwater world the admiration it deserves … wouldn't it be wonderful to dive in? The landscape of your jarrarium will grow and reach a balance over time.

ALGAE
Remove surface scum to keep bacteria levels down. Floating plants also help with this. I like to add small nerite snails to clean algae off the glass. Freshwater shrimp are also a good idea; like the snails, they fertilise the plants with their manure. Direct light can cause algal blooms.

WATER
Top up the water every other week, as it evaporates. Plants purify the water, thereby reducing tank maintenance.

LIGHT
Place your jarrarium in bright, indirect light.

MAINTENANCE
Prune plants and remove any dead leaves.

PROJECT
8

PLANT
PARENTHOOD

PLANT PARENTHOOD

PROPAGATING PLANTS

—

Not having an outdoor garden was a blessing in disguise; it focused my gardening aspirations inside the house, eventually providing me with my dream job. Once I understood the optimal environment and needs of my different plants, an indoor garden was the perfect fit. However, every spring finds me gazing longingly out of the window, greedy for more green and a garden of my own.

Propagating plants is such a happy pursuit, and thankfully the best time for rooting cuttings is in the spring. Creating new growth from cuttings will save you money, once you have invested in all the lovely little glass bottles and vases. They will look ever so pretty lined up on a windowsill or mantelpiece and they take the edge off any garden-craving, green-eyed monsters.

Water can be used to root cuttings of easily propagated species. Some plants will not respond well to this method. I have listed below some tried-and-tested species that should perform beautifully, but try this out on the plant du jour that has you smitten. It may not work, but just imagine if it does?

YOU WILL NEED

A SHARP KNIFE OR SCISSORS

CLEAR GLASS VESSELS

ROOM-TEMPERATURE WATER

CUTTINGS TO TRY:
Devil's ivy (*Epipremnum aureum*)
Heart-leafed philodendron (*Philodendron cordatum*)
African violets (*Saintpaulia spp.*)
Coleus (*Plectranthus scutellarioides*)
Begonia (*Begonia rex*)
Spider plant (*Chlorophytum comosum*)
Geranium (*Pelargonium × hortorum*)
English ivy (*Hedera helix*)
Peppermint (*Mentha × piperita*)
Basil (*Ocimum basilicum*)

METHOD

1. Make a clean angled cut around 10cm from the tip of the stem, above a leaf node or, if not a trailing plant, cut the leaf from the plant at its base.

2. Fill clear glass vessels with room-temperature water.

3. Add the plantlets, ensuring around half of each cutting is above the water and extends beyond the vessel's lip. No leaves from the cuttings should be submerged in water.

4. Place in bright, indirect light.

5. Change the water every day, keeping it free from nasties. This will also prevent the stem rotting.

6. Once roots have developed, you can transplant into little pots filled with potting soil. Burrow a hole, plant and tamp down soil around roots. You will need to nurture the plant whilst it becomes established. Keep the soil moist and the plant shaded for a while as the plant adapts to soil after being in water. Repot when the plant outgrows its small pot.

PROJECT

9

FAMILY
PLANNING

FAMILY
PLANNING

SUCCULENT PROPAGATION MANDALAS

—

It's so easy to grow succulents and this rewarding activity, as you become broody for new plants, will provide you with the thrill of fostering and nurturing succulent buds. There are a few different ways of propagating succulents and in this task we will be using leaves, creating a prettily patterned mandala by arranging the leaves in a circular design.

MANDALA

The word 'mandala' comes from Sanskrit and means circle or wholeness. These geometric patterns are representative of the universe and are used as objects to focus on whilst meditating.

Propagating succulents from leaves is a lengthy process and will take some time. Creating a mandala is a beautiful way to continue the circle of life and arrange succulent leaves while waiting for some tiny roots to appear.

—

*'A mandala is the psychological expression
of the totality of the self.'*
CARL JUNG

YOU WILL NEED

YOUR FAVOURITE SUCCULENTS

PLATE
(to initially lay out and dry leaves)

TRAY OR POT (TO ARRANGE YOUR MANDALA IN)
(sturdy enough to hold soil, with a wide enough
diameter to create your design)

SOIL
(regular potting soil or succulent soil)

WATER MISTER

POT
(to plant the baby succulents)

TERRARIUM TOOLKIT (PAGE 17)

METHOD

1   Pluck some leaves from your favourite succulents,
    wiggling them back and forth. Ensure you snap
    off the entire leaf.

2   Place them on a tray and leave out for a few
    days in the shade, until they have dried out. This
    will allow the ends to callus or heal over. Plonking
    them directly onto soil can cause them to rot.

3   They can now be moved to your allocated
    mandala tray or pot. Fill around 5–10cm deep
    with soil. It's time to get imaginative with your
    circular design. Organise your leaves into shapes
    and colours and create your magical mandala.

4   Place your completed mandala where it can get
    ample indirect sunlight.

5   Give leaves a good mist every couple of days,
    when the soil has dried out. Do not add water if
    the soil feels moist.

6   Be patient, leaves can sprout roots within a week
    or a couple of months! In the meantime, you have
    a beautiful mandala to meditate over whilst you
    eagerly anticipate their arrival.

7   Hurray! Hairy roots have started to sprout. In
    time, adorable little buds will emerge at the leaf's
    base. The leaf's work is done and it's time for the
    baby succulent to take over. They will eventually
    separate from one another; you may need to give
    them a little nudge if they're holding on.

8   The babies are now ready to be planted in their
    own new homes. Add some succulent soil to a
    pot with drainage and make a little hole with
    your finger or bamboo stick.

9   Nestle your succulent in gently, by tamping down
    soil around the roots. Keep an eye on them as
    they start to grow and water them weekly.

PLANT
-O-
SAURUS

PLANT-O-SAURUS

GOLD DINOSAUR PLANTER

—

Well, haven't we been very grown up until now? Projects introducing small and big kids alike to the delights of planting can be very rewarding and this is one of my favourites.

A cheerful spin on old toys can bring them out of retirement. This is quite a simple, but addictive task. Before you know it, you'll find yourself wandering around charity shops, eyeing up toys, weighing up whether they'd look handsome with a cactus growing out of their back or whether they can enhance your current menagerie of divine planters. They also make super gifts.

YOU WILL NEED

HOLLOW PLASTIC TOY
(dinosaurs, dolls, trolls, farm animals etc.)

SHARP CRAFT KNIFE OR POWER DRILL
(if the plastic is very hard)

MULTI-PURPOSE SURFACE PRIMER

METALLIC SPRAY PAINT

SMALL STONES OR PEBBLES FOR DRAINAGE

SUCCULENT / CACTI SOIL

SUCCULENTS OR CACTI

CARE

Succulents do very well indoors in a bright spot — give them a few pipettes of water when the soil feels completely dry to the touch.

METHOD

1 This plastic T Rex is donating his body to horticultural science ... meet Bolan. If you are working with very hard plastic, you may find it easier to drill into Bolan's back. Most hollow toys have a bit of give and a craft knife should suffice. Carefully slice through the plastic on Bolan's back, creating an opening and revealing the hollow cavity within. Ensure the hole is large enough to fit a small plant or two in. With the knife, try to smooth out any frays in the plastic.

2 In a well-ventilated area, spray Bolan with a surface primer and let him dry. Time to pimp up Bolan with a couple of evenly sprayed, metallic coats. Allow him to dry between sprays and completely overnight.

3 For drainage, add small stones or pebbles to his hollow feet and a very thin layer covering his lower belly.

4 Add succulent potting soil, leaving space below the hole for your plant. Remove plants from their pots, and loosen off soil.

5 Transplant into Bolan's back. Pat down soil to secure and add more if needed.

THESE
REALLY ARE
MAGICAL

THESE REALLY
ARE MAGICAL

MUSHROOMS

—

Unless I am holding a fairy-garden kids' workshop, which often requires the additional input of figurines and waterfalls, I like to focus primarily on the plants when creating terrariums. That being said, I have always enjoyed including treasured natural elements like crystals and fossils.

I have recently become a little obsessed with mushrooms. What is it about the little fellas that instantly connect us to the fairy tales of our youth and an idyllic childhood notion of the woods?

YOU WILL NEED

POLYMER / OVEN-BAKE CLAY IN WHITE OR TAUPE TONE
(such as Fimo from your local artshop)

TOOTHPICK (OPTIONAL)

SILVER FLORAL OR FINE WIRE

BAKING TRAY

GOLD OR SILVER SPRAY PAINT AND FOIL (OPTIONAL)

METHOD

1 Roll balls of polymer or clay into different lengths, skinnier at one end than at the other. The skinnier end is your stalk or stem and the more bulbous side is the mushroom's cap.

2 Begin to shape the mushroom's cap. You can also add gills underneath the cap with a toothpick or piece of wire. Mushrooms often have a frayed ring halfway down their stem, which you may like to sculpt. I usually stylise my mushrooms, making them a little simpler to create.

3 Fold wire in half. You should have enough wire once doubled to fit halfway up the stem of your mushroom, with roughly the same amount coming out of the mushroom's base. These are your mushroom's roots and will anchor it into the soil.

4 Very gently, press the flattened folded end of the wire into the base, pushing it straight up the stem. Hopefully the wire doesn't pop out randomly as you are pushing it in.

5 Place your mushrooms on the baking tray, pop them in the oven and bake following the instructions on the packaging. Let the mushrooms cool once cooked.

6 Get creative with metallic spray paint and foil, if you like. Gild them completely or splatter them with a few spatters of sparkle. If you like a more natural look keep them plain or try to replicate the fly agaric (*Amanita muscaria*). This archetypical toadstool often depicted in Enid Blyton books and fairy tales is deep red with white spots. The clay varieties are without the hallucinogenic properties of the real thing, but they still have the same magical appearance and don't mind if you never water them.

7 Gather the mushrooms together in little clusters; they will add charm to your Tropical or Orchid Terrarium.

—

INTERESTING FACT

DNA studies show fungi are more closely related to humans than to plants.

IT'S A
CONCRETE JUNGLE
OUT THERE

IT'S A CONCRETE JUNGLE OUT THERE

MAKE A CONCRETE PLANTER

—

I find the bustling city irresistible. There's nowhere better to explore the cracks, crevices, fissures and faults, where nature intrudes into the sharp lines of cement blocks. Plants and concrete butt against one another, constantly testing each other's boundaries.

One of my favourite places to visit in London is the conservatory at the Barbican. This hidden gem juxtaposes Brutalist architecture with lush green foliage. Drawing inspiration from the concrete jungle, we'll be faceting planters from cement, providing succulents or cacti with chic urban dwellings. Photocopy the template or visit my website www.alysonmowat.com for a selection of designs to choose from.

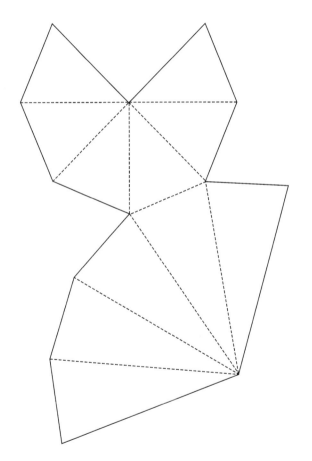

YOU WILL NEED

SPRAY MOUNT

GEM TEMPLATE (LEFT),
scaled up and photocopied 300 per cent to A3 size or
download full-size templates at www.alysonmowat.com

3MM FOAM BOARD

CRAFT KNIFE

SELLOTAPE

HEAVY-DUTY TAPE / ELECTRICAL TAPE / CARPET TAPE

VERY SMALL SUCCULENT OR CACTUS AND THE PLASTIC
POT IT CAME IN (NO BIGGER THAN 4CM DIAMETER)

CLING FILM

QUICK-SETTING CEMENT

BUCKET OR BOWL

FINE SANDPAPER

METHOD

1 Spray mount your photocopied or printed template to the foam board.

2 Cut completely around the solid line.

3 Now score the dashed lines, ensuring you do not push the knife all the way through the foam board.

4 Bend against the score, keeping the inner lining of the foam board intact. Manoeuvre the structure into shape, securing it in key points with sellotape. You should see your shape coming together nicely with one of the planes missing; it's not a mistake. Ensure your pot fits easily within the missing plane.

5 Secure the shape with heavy-duty tape, firming up the structure and concentrating on all the weak areas. It will start to look a bit messy on the outside, but it's essential to keep everything intact and structurally strong when we start to pour in the cement.

6 Remove the plant and soil from the pot. Cover the pot inside and out with cling film.

7 Put the cement in a bucket or bowl, preferably one with a lip that will allow you to pour the liquid. Following the instructions on the cement packaging, mix up a gloopy paste. Keep stirring, mixing in any clumps. You will need to work quickly as the cement dries surprisingly fast.

8 Spoon some of the mixture into the open plane and swirl around the inside of the structure, testing that there are no weak points. If you feel cement oozing through gaps, add more tape.

9 Now pour in your mixture. Hold the mould at an angle, so that the opening is flat and horizontal. Fill up with cement until you reach half a centimetre below the opening.

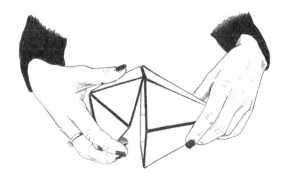

10 Now push your cling-filmed pot into the cement, so that the top of the pot is in line with the surface of the cement. Now tape the pot down, as it is inclined to pop out otherwise. Leave your planter to dry overnight. I usually remove the inner pot after a few hours; whilst there is still a bit of give in the cement, as it can be difficult to pull it out when the cement is solid.

11 The following day, pull off the tape and foam board for the big reveal; it's a lovely feeling. Rub any rough planes back and forth against fine flat sandpaper, emphasising facets and angles. Most of the planter will be smooth, but the area that usually needs work is the open plane, as the concrete often settles at a different level without the same clean, flat line. Your planter is ready to be planted with soil and a cactus or succulent.

CARE

Add water sparingly with a pipette, as there is no drainage hole.

HUNG
UP
ON
YOU

HUNG UP ON YOU

MACRAMÉ HANGING PLANTER

—

By this time you'll have terrariums and planters on every shelf. I know what it's like to run out of prime planting space and you may well find your gaze shifting upwards. What could possibly be better than the addition of a hanging garden? For these planters we'll be glamming up natural macramé cord, using silk rope instead. The key feature of this design is the romantic Josephine knot, a linking knot that is frequently referred to as the lover's knot.

YOU WILL NEED

BRASS RING

12 METRES OF SILK ROPE
(you can find this at your local haberdashery)

SCISSORS

MEASURING TAPE

POT

ELASTIC BAND

BEADS OR BRASS ENDS
(from a hardware shop or plumbing supplier – optional)

MELTED WAX OR A GLUE GUN TO SEAL FRAYED ENDS
(OPTIONAL)

METHOD

1. Find a good place to work and hang up your ring; I hang the brass ring from a favourite door handle, sitting cross-legged on the floor, but you may prefer to stand with the ring hung higher up.

2. Cut four 2.5m lengths of silk rope, trying not to get too tangled up. There's usually one rebel strand in the bunch, so once the first length is cut, measure the other ends against the first. If they start to unravel, tape the ends.

3. Cut the leftover rope in half. This will be used to secure the top and bottom of your planter.

4. Thread all four ropes through the ring, up to their halfway point. They've multiplied and you should now have eight ropes to work with. Time to do a gathering knot, to secure the ring in place.

Gathering knot

5 Take one piece of your leftover silk rope
and make a 'u' loop to the left of the ropes,
just below the ring.

6 Cross left end of loop over the right, continue
over the silk rope. Wrap it over and around the
group of silk rope and the loop. Wrap tightly
around the entire loop and group approximately
10 times.

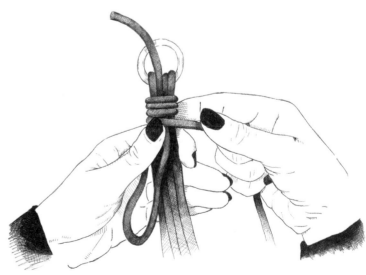

7 Once wrapped, take your rope's end and thread it through the loop at the bottom, then pull both ends in opposite directions. Keep pulling until the loop is tucked inside the wrap. Cut the ends, tucking them into the rope sheath.

8 Bravo ... your first knot is tied, time to make way for Josie.

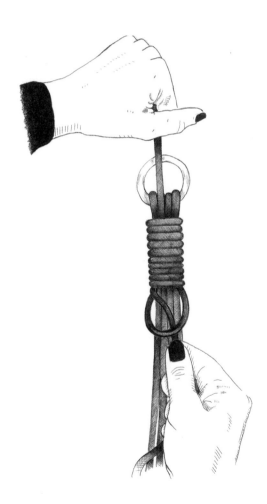

Josephine knot

9 Start the first pair of Josephine knots about 60cm below the gathering knot. Divide the silk cords into two groups of four strands and tie one group to the side to keep them out of the way.

10 Divide your group of four ropes into two sets; left and right. Take the left set and loop it under itself.

11 Take your right set and place it over the loop of the left set, then under the loose strands of the left set. Try to bear with me for the next bit... it may take a bit of practice, but it's essentially over-under-over-under, diagonally from left to right. We will only be moving the right set in the next few steps.

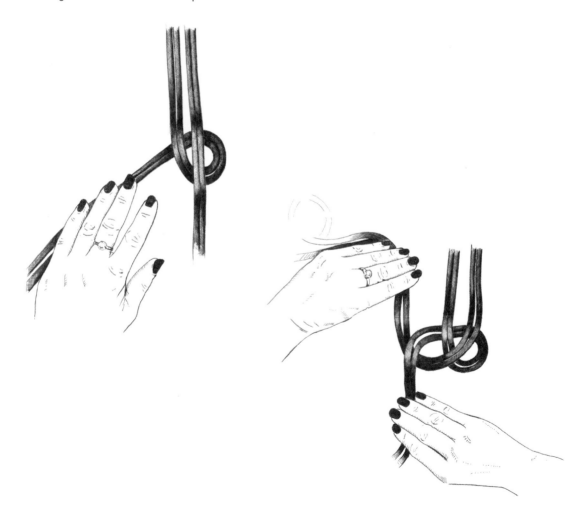

12 Still with the right set, place it over the straight strands coming from the gathering knot, then under the left set (where the loop is). The right set then goes over itself (where it first passed over the loop) and then under the loop of the left set.

13 You will need to do some manoeuvring. Tighten the knot by pulling the ends. Then untie the other group and repeat steps 9–12.

14 Once you've tied both knots, turn the ring
around and repeat the step with the second
group, ensuring that the knot is at the same
level as the first.

15 Leave a gap of about 10cm and tie two more
Josephine knots, splitting the groups you made
previously.

16 Now take your pot and position it between
the Josephine knots, securing it below with
an elastic band.

17 Take the last piece of rope and tie another
gathering knot just below the elastic band.
Cut and remove the elastic band.

18 Finish rope ends with brass hardware or beads,
if you like. You can then dip ends in wax or seal
with a glue gun to stop them from fraying. Plant
something magnificent in a pot or kokedama
and hang to show off your newfound knack
for knotting.

CARE

When watering plants, remove them from the
macramé hanging planter. Ensure they have
sufficiently drip-dried before returning them.

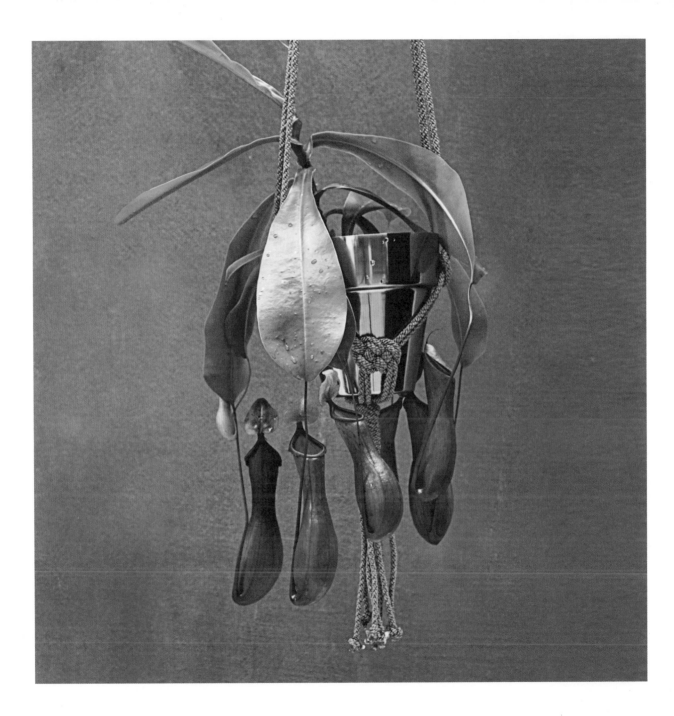

PROJECT
14

STICK
'EM
UP

STICK 'EM UP

STAG-HORN FERN MOUNTING

—

Staghorn ferns (*Platycerium spp.*) get their name from the staghorn deer, whose forked antlers bear a resemblance to the majestic fronds of these exquisite ferns.

Staghorn ferns are epiphytes. Their roots keep a tight grip, allowing them to cling onto other plants or trees in their natural habitat. Like the epiphytic orchids we encountered in Project 5, staghorn ferns are happiest when exposing their extremities to the elements. They absorb nutrients and moisture in their fronds.

In this task, I'll be mounting a staghorn fern onto a wooden plaque, a playful take on old hunting trophies, but completely suitable for vegans. I must stress, no plants were harmed in the mounting of these staghorn ferns!

YOU WILL NEED

STAGHORN FERN
You can detach the side growths, or pups, from a well-established plant or purchase young plants from a nursery

CONSTRUCTION STAPLE GUN

FISHING LINE

WOODEN TROPHY SHIELD MOUNTING PLAQUE, OR ANY OLD WOODEN BOARD, SLICE OF TREE TRUNK, SPLIT LOG, REPURPOSED PALLET TRAY – GET CREATIVE!

SPHAGNUM MOSS (*SPHAGNUM SPP.*)

HOOK SCREWS AND STRING FOR HANGING TO A WALL

METHOD

1 Remove the staghorn fern from its pot and gently remove any potting medium, whilst loosening the plant's root system.

2 Staple the fishing line to the back of the mount. You may need to staple a few times to secure the line. Turn the mount over.

3 Moisten a handful of sphagnum moss and add it onto the mount, which should be lying flat on a surface in front of you.

4 Push down on the plate of your fern, so that it makes contact with the moss. Add a little more sphagnum on top of the roots, to protect them when you start wrapping.

5 Begin to wrap tightly around the plaque and fern plate with the securely stapled fishing line, ensuring you don't get any fronds caught up in all the commotion. Keep wrapping until the fern feels secure.

6 Staple the end of the line onto the back on the plaque. The fishing line will disappear from view in time as the fern begins to grow.

7 Now it's ready to hang up; screw in the hook screw, thread some string through and voilà; you can adorn your wall.

CARE

LIGHT

Avoid direct sunlight; these plants will thrive in bright indirect light.

MOISTURE

Keep humidity high by misting with distilled water once a day. When fronds are looking droopy, you will need to give the shield fronds (the plate-like fronds that protect the roots) as well as the roots a proper watering by submerging the plant in a bucket of purified water for 10 minutes. Hold on to the plaque so that everything gets submerged in the water apart from the wooden base. Allow the plant to dry out completely between baths.

AIR

They like to be in a well-ventilated, airy spot.

LEAVES

Avoid wiping the leaves, as this will remove the silvery velvet surface.

FEEDING

You will need to feed your staghorn fern monthly during the warmer seasons (spring and summer) and every other month in colder dormant periods (autumn and winter). Use a water-soluble, all-purpose fertiliser.

TIP

Banana peel is high in potassium and will benefit sensitive staghorns by helping to remove some of the damaging sodium found in water. Make banana water by soaking the skin overnight. Use this magical potion when spraying or submerging your plant in water.

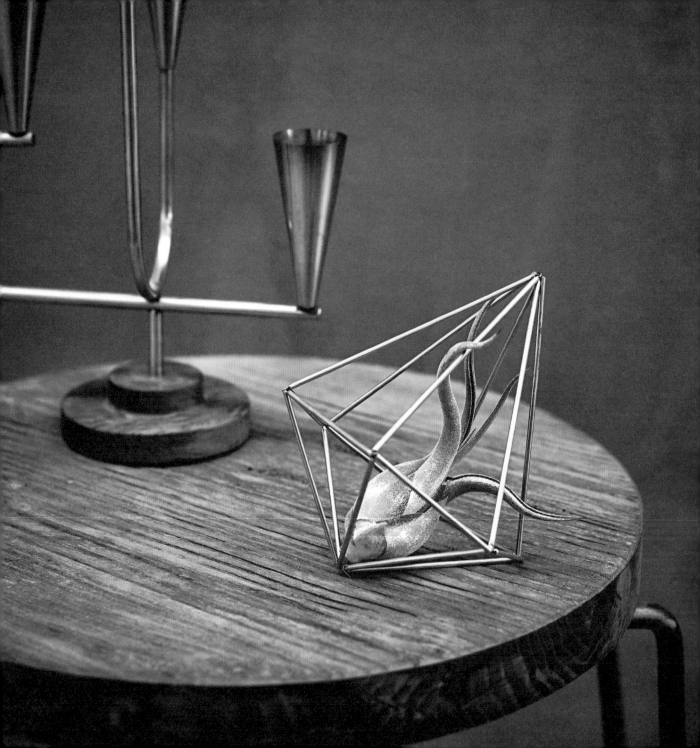

LIVING ON
LOVE
AND
FRESH AIR

LIVING ON LOVE AND FRESH AIR

COPPER HIMMELI AIR PLANT HOLDER

—

Himmeli are a Finnish holiday decoration, traditionally made from pieces of straw in an attempt to secure a bounteous crop for the following year. The larger and more elaborate the sculpture, the greater the crop. We will be replacing straw with copper piping, so that the structure can happily prop up and nuzzle an air plant. Here's hoping our himmeli-inspired jewel-shaped talismans bring an abundance of sparkle and delight over the coming year.

This diamond is a good place to start (aren't they always?), but once you've developed the knack, experiment with other geometric structures. They make beautiful mobiles when massed together, and can be hung, mounted or simply placed on a shelf or table; the possibilities are endless. Explore the relationship between the plant and the brass structure, experimenting with different angles.

YOU WILL NEED

COPPER PIPING (6–8MM DIAMETER)
(found in the plumbing section of hardware stores)

SILVER FLORAL OR FINE WIRE
(thin enough to thread through the diameter of the copper pipe and back again)

MINI HACKSAW OR SMALL 'TUBE CUTTER'

MITRE BOX
(not necessary if you have a tube cutter)

RULER

WIRE CUTTERS

AIRPLANT
Caput Medusae, Ionantha Scaposa or an airplant species that fits within your finished himmeli

—

TIP

If you can't get hold of brass tubing, try using drinking straws instead; link them together with a needle and thread and spray-paint with metallic paint once constructed.

METHOD

1   Measure and cut 18 sections of copper piping; six measuring 10cm long, six measuring 6cm and six 5cm long.

2   Cut around 2m thin wire and kink at one end. At the other end start to thread through three tubes – first one 10cm, then one 5cm and finally another 10cm.

3   Connect them in a triangle shape. Twist the end wire (with the kink) and main wire together.

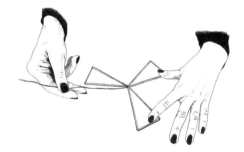

4   Repeat adding another 10 × 5 × 10cm triangle. Wrap the main wire around the tip of the first triangle, linking the two.

5   Now you are ready for your third 10 × 5 × 10cm triangle, again connecting it with the tips of the other two. Your tube and wirework should resemble the three sails of a windmill.

6   The main wire will now be in the centre. Thread it backwards through one of the 10cm tubes.

7   Now add a couple of 6cm tubes, thread backwards through the 5cm tube, adding another triangle to your sail.

8 Add a 5cm tube and wrap wire around the closest corner of your next triangle.

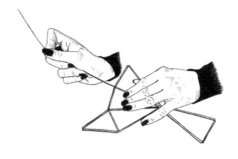

9 Add two 6cm tubes and wrap twice around. Add a 5cm tube and wrap twice around the next triangle. The shape of your structure should be changing, making it more three-dimensional.

10 Add your final two 6cm tubes, wrap and add a 5cm tube. Now push the wire from the bottom up, through the next 6cm tube, closing the structure.

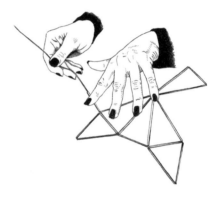

11 Now bring all your smaller points together in the centre and wrap them together with the wire at the diamond's point. Cut and tuck the excess wire into one of the pipes.

12 Now it's ready to add your plant.

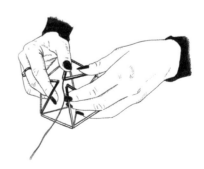

CARING FOR YOUR AIR PLANT

Air plants (*Tillandsia spp.*) are curious little fellas. Unusual in the sense that they absorb nutrients through their leaves and don't require soil to bed roots into. Their looks also make them stand out in a crowd. Who could deny their quirky style (they are relatives of the pineapple after all), all spiky foliage and out there, not to mention the pop of purple and pink blooms that appeal to hummingbirds and butterflies in their natural environment.

Their lack of a need for soil makes air plants ideal for ornamental display and the perfect partner for our diamond himmeli project.

Air plants love the light, but nothing too direct. They like it breezy, so avoid enclosing them in a terrarium or tight corner. Mist every couple of days and give them a good bath, though never in icy water, once a fortnight. Leave them bopping along leisurely for around half an hour. Avoid handling them too much as this will affect the silvery coating that is essential for the proper functioning of air plants.

PROJECT
16

BONSAI
LIKE
MR MIYAGI

BONSAI LIKE MR MIYAGI

CLOSE YOUR EYES, CONCENTRATE.
THINK ONLY TREE...

—

Grey gardens

I'll sometimes catch myself peering into the future, imagining my golden days, white bun on top of my head, held in place by a couple of chopsticks or a paintbrush. Draped in a kimono, I'll be tending to my plants and menagerie of exotic animals. I used to refer to these as my 'bonsai years', because this was the time when I planned to invest in a few saplings to tend and manipulate into imitating the majestic trees that I would have encountered in my youth.

However, I have since realised that if I want to truly enjoy the pruned miniatures of my mind's eye... well, I had better get cracking. To be a true bonsai master you must first accept that infinite patience is your greatest virtue.

About bonsai

Bonsai means 'plant in a tray' and is the ancient Japanese art of stunting a tree's growth by skilful pruning. The tree is prohibited from developing by keeping it in a small container.

When you begin to bonsai, you are shaping the idea of a tree that belongs somewhere in the future. Bonsai are often passed down through generations as heirlooms, leaving a legacy of hope, serenity and grace.

It is possible to bonsai almost any tree. It is a common misconception that Bonsai are breeds of miniature trees or teacup variety plants or have genetic dwarfing properties, but the only changes made are those implemented by the human hand.

Most bonsai are outdoorsy types. They are trees, after all, and want to feel the sunshine on their leaves. Alfresco trees include pine (*Pinus spp.*), maple (*Acer spp.*) and larch (*Larix spp.*), to name but a few. My favourite outdoor tree to start on is the juniper tree (*Juniperus spp.*). Examples of bonsai that can be grown indoors include fig trees (*Ficus spp.*), scorpion bush (*Carmona spp.*) and Chinese elm (*Ulmus parvifolia*).

POTTING

—

Selecting your tree

You can grow from seed, however, if you do, prepare for a lot of watching paint dry. I would personally recommend buying a small plant or tree from your local nursery or, even better, get in touch with your local bonsai club, they usually have trees to sell and love to talk bonsai.

Like a sculptor about to chisel out a form in stone, ask yourself, does your tree possess the bare bones of what you envisage for it? Try to select a tree that grows well in your area. Avoid trees that already look wizened and aged, it's up to you to style the tree, making it appear older than its years.

Harmony is key in considering the tree you want to emulate. I've started to bonsai a tree inspired by one my brother and I were photographed in front of in Vancouver a few years ago. Tending to this bonsai reminds me of our bond, despite now living on opposite sides of the world. He also loves and respects trees more than any person I know and we often send photos to one another of the beautiful and unusual trees we encounter along the way.

Selecting your pot

Literally anything with drainage holes (the Japanese call these 'eyes') or that can be drilled can be repurposed as a bonsai container. Your bonsai tree will always be chasing the limelight but aim to find balance and proportion between the tree and the vessel that contains it.

Consider style

There are different styles of bonsai and they are named according to their shape and angle of the trunk. Although I would encourage you to freestyle your bonsai moves, working with the tree and what it wants to do, there are some traditional styles you may wish to follow.

- Formal upright bonsai style (Chokkan)
- Informal upright bonsai style (Moyogi)
- Slanting bonsai style (Shakan)
- Cascade bonsai style (Kengai)
- Semi-cascade bonsai style (Han-kengai)

YOU WILL NEED

POT WITH ONE OR MORE DRAINAGE HOLES

DRAINAGE MESH, CUT INTO A SQUARE LARGER
THAN THE DRAINAGE HOLE

ANODISED ALUMINIUM WIRE AND WIRE CUTTER

AKADAMA SOIL OR CAT LITTER
(low-dust, fired-clay granules)

BONSAI SOIL
You can purchase a pre-mixed bonsai soil or create
your own depending on your tree's specific needs

TREE
I chose a small juniper (the 'Karate Kid' tree
made famous by the movie)

FORK

WOODEN CHOPSTICKS

WET SPHAGNUM MOSS (SPHAGNUM SPP.)

METHOD

1   To prevent soil from dropping out of the drainage
    hole, cover the pot on the inside with the mesh.
    Bend a 10cm piece of wire into a U shape.
    Push the ends through the mesh, then bend open
    against the bottom of the pot.

2   Bend a long piece of wire into another U. Thread
    the ends up through the mesh. Open them to
    opposite sides of the pot, then push them down
    flush with the pot. This will help anchor and
    secure the tree.

3   Add a thin drainage layer of akadama soil or cat
    litter, then a thin layer of bonsai soil, at least 1cm
    deep. Set aside.

4   Remove the plant from its nursery pot; you may
    need to cut into the pot to separate it from the
    plant and soil. Tease out the roots gently with a
    fork or your fingers. Using horizontal strokes with
    a wooden chopstick, gently remove the soil from
    the top surface, revealing the roots.

5   Trim off excess and damaged roots from the root
    ball with neat little snips all the way around,
    ensuring that there are no flyaway roots and your
    root ball is a clearly defined structure.

6   Place the tree into the new pot, on top of the thin
    soil layers. Add soil up the sides. Press down on
    soil and push chopsticks through the soil at the
    side of the root ball, to fill out any air pockets.

7   Twist the side wires together tightly in the centre,
    pull and then twist again to secure the tree into
    the pot. Be careful not to cause any damage.

8   Water the tree thoroughly, ideally with rainwater,
    then add clumps of wet sphagnum, covering the
    surface of the soil, and flatten evenly.

WIRING

—

The aim of wiring is to clearly define the branches and to create space around the main trunk, giving the tree more character and visual appeal. Wire is like braces for trees, it guides rather than interrupts growth, allowing you to reposition the branches.

YOU WILL NEED

ANODISED ALUMINIUM WIRE
(you will need a range of sizes, but start with 3mm)

WIRE CUTTER

METHOD

1   Identify a branch that needs manoeuvering.

2   Cut a piece of wire long enough to tackle the branch. Anchor the wire with your thumb onto the trunk, wrap around the trunk with your other hand, before moving up to the branch. Wrap at a 45-degree angle around the branch, bending the wired branch into position as you wrap.

3   Snip the wire with the cutters when you have finished wrapping.

4   Over time you will get a feeling for how flexible your tree is and how much pressure you can apply.

5   Remove the wire if it starts to look tight and before the wire grows into the branch and scars the tree. Then rewire.

CARING FOR YOUR LITTLE ONE

WEATHER

Avoid strong sun in the summer and protect from freezing temperatures in the winter.

WATER

Bonsai are big drinkers and become parched without enough H_2O. In summer you may need to water your bonsai daily. Lift the moss and push your finger a couple of centimetres into the soil. If it feels dry, fill a bucket or bowl with water. Lower your bonsai pot into the water, ensuring the water level isn't higher than the moss covering the soil. Allow it to sit for a while, sucking up the water from below. When the sphagnum moss starts to darken, becoming damp, remove the pot from the bowl of water. Trees growing indoors in centrally heated apartments require misting all over with water daily.

REPOTTING

Carefully repot in early spring if necessary. If you notice roots pushing out of the bottom of the pot, pull out your tree a little and if you see roots circling outside of the soil, it's time to repot. Apologise profusely as you trim roots, cutting off around a third of the outer root ball. You can start in a new pot, or you can repot in the same container.

PRUNING

Your tree will really be testing its boundaries over the summer months. Practise passive plant-parenting at your own peril.

Consider negative space and 'leave room for the birds to fly through'*.
Trim any branches and leaves that are not part of your plan, thinning out dense areas to allow air to reach the inner branches. Trees are very forgiving, so be bold, Edward Scissorhands.

Rub away or cut off buds that are not required. I like to make any big structural changes in early spring, but continue to snip and refine the shape of my trees until early autumn.

*John Naka – master bonsai cultivator

A
TOUCH
OF
KOKE-DRAMA

A TOUCH OF KOKE-DRAMA

HOW TO MAKE KOKEDAMA

—

Liberate your plants! Take your green thumb to dizzying new heights where moss is boss and terracotta pots have fallen from grace. Snuggle roots in a duvet of moss, cat litter (wha-at?!) and mud before binding in twine and dangling from a hook.

Kokedama translates as 'moss ball' from Japanese, and is also dubbed the 'poor man's bonsai'. It's tied into the same ancient practice and remains popular in Japanese gardens today.

If you would rather not string up a hanging garden in your home, display kokedama on altar-like stands (see pages 128–131) and arrange in artistic groupings. Either way, the results are extraordinarily appealing.

YOU WILL NEED

GLOVES (IT'S GOING TO GET MESSY)

PLANT
Moss loves moisture, so complement it with a plant you might include in a tropical terrarium (see page 18). I often use asparagus ferns but other kokedama superstars include philodendrons (*Philodendron spp.*), pothos plant (*Epipremnum aureum*), begonias (*Begonia spp.*) and bromeliads (Bromeliaceae).

COTTON THREAD

MOISTENED SPHAGNUM MOSS (*SPHAGNUM SPP.*)

POTTING SOIL

AKADAMA SOIL OR CAT LITTER
Akadama is pricey and can be hard to come by. I've discovered that some cat litter products have the same consistency as this granular clay, draining well but also helping to bind the soil. Go for a low-dust, lightweight cat litter and invest in a beautiful plant instead.

SHEET MOSS (*HYPNUM SPP*), ENOUGH TO WRAP THE MUDDY SPHERE

SCISSORS

TWINE

BUCKET

METHOD

1. Don your gloves and pull the plant from its pot. Gently remove as much soil as possible, so that the roots are exposed.

2. Using cotton thread, lightly tie some moistened sphagnum moss around the roots of the plant, for some extra cushioning. The cotton will eventually dissolve. Put your plant to one side.

3. Mix together 7 handfuls of potting soil and 3 handfuls of akadama soil or cat litter. Add water until the mud is sticky but holds together. Do your best to form a firm ball from the mix as large as your hands can comfortably manage. Squeeze out any excess water. Save some soil mixture to patch up any cracks.

4. Carefully break your soil ball in half, then gently press your plant's root clump inside.

5. Close the halves back into a sphere, patching up the split with the excess soil. It's a little tricky holding it all together, and you'll wish you were an octopus with a few extra limbs. Don't panic when cracks appear and bits of soil slip through your fingers – no drama, it's normal.

6. Press sections of sheet moss around the sphere. Try not to leave any open spaces and cut off excess folds.

7. Holding the moss ball in one hand, use your other hand to wrap the twine around in a criss-cross pattern, turning the moss ball continuously. Do this until all the moss feels securely wrapped.

8. To finish, secure with a knot and cut off any excess twine. If you decide to hang your kokedama, tie two lengths of twine either side of the moss ball and suspend from a hook.

CARE

Kokedama are not carefree. Weekly bathing, maintaining humidity and finding
a good home for your moss ball are all key to avoiding any koke-drama.

LIGHT
Bright indoor position, avoid direct sunlight.

WATER
Water when leaves show signs of wilting or when the kokedama feels light.
As a general rule, bathe once a week for around 10 minutes, by placing the moss
ball in a bucket or sink of water. Drain excess water and when it's no longer dripping,
the kokedama is ready for display again. Foliage will appreciate regular mistings.
I like to do my misting in the morning when the sun is not likely to fry leaves.

PROJECT
18

INSIDE
OUT

INSIDE OUT

AND ROUND AND ROUND KOKEDAMA

—

Avoid scrunching up orchid roots in a kokedama ball. An epiphyte's roots do not appreciate being tightly packed and will demand their freedom. Instead, you can trick nature's ultimate trickster into enjoying the swinging heights of a kokedama, by turning our usual kokedama recipe inside out!

YOU WILL NEED

SPHAGNUM MOSS (*SPHAGNUM SPP.*),
placed in a bucket and saturated with rainwater

A MESHED FRUIT OR VEGETABLE BAG

RUBBER BANDS

BOWL

WOOD CHIPS

EPIPHYTIC ORCHID

FISHING WIRE

CARE

See epiphytic orchid (page 39). When watering, dunk weekly in room-temperature water, rather than bathe. Mist daily.

METHOD

1 Open out the mesh bag, wrap a rubber band around one side and turn the 'bag' inside out.

2 In a bowl mix a few handfuls of the sphagnum moss with the wood chips and pat together in your hands. Shape into a ball and push it into the mesh bag. Close the mesh around its contents, making a sphere, and tie or secure with a rubber band. Cut off the excess mesh.

3 Place the orchid on top and drape its roots around the ball. If your orchid came clipped to a stick, you can use this to anchor the roots onto the sphere, but avoid damaging them.

4 Take handfuls of the wet moss, squeezing it out, and wrap it around the sphere with fishing wire to cover the unsightly mesh, being careful not to decapitate flowers or trap leaves.

5 That's a wrap! Hang upside-down, place the right way around in a kokedama stand (see pages 128–131), or whichever other way that takes your fancy.

PROJECT
19

KAWAII!

KAWAII!

JAPANESE STAND FOR KOKEDAMA

—

Not all of us have the perfect spot to dangle kokedama, so some prefer to let them perch. Others like to alleviate any possibility of a head-on collision with a mossy sphere. I like to make my own bowl-shaped stands to nestle moss balls when they are not hovering above me.

The marble paper often used in bookbinding inspires one of my favourite methods of doing this. I love the look and smell of old books. It's a delight to uncover them, in the musty recesses of an antiquarian bookshop, bearing marbled covers or endpapers.

Wherever possible in my planting, I like to link or reference other obsessions – be it crystals, books, fossils, taxidermy, enchanted worlds or cabinets of curiosities. Plants, for me, keep these passions alive and often provide the perfect backdrop or protagonist. Perhaps this is something you would like to consider when curating your own botanical collection.

YOU WILL NEED

POLYMER / OVEN-BAKE CLAY
IN A SELECTION OF COLOURS

NON-STICK ROLLING PIN

CLING FILM

COMPASS TO MEASURE OUT TEMPLATE

TRACING PAPER

CRAFT KNIFE

OLIVE OIL

SMALL OVEN-SAFE BOWL

SANDPAPER (OPTIONAL)

METALLIC LIQUID GILDING PAINT AND
SMALL PAINTBRUSH (OPTIONAL)

SILVER OR GOLD FOIL PAPER (OPTIONAL)

GLAZE TO SEAL DISH (OPTIONAL)

METHOD

1 Roll different colours of clay into little chipolata-like shapes. Don't worry too much about measurements, although I like to include larger rolls of white, black or grey. Anything left over can be wrapped and used again.

2 To combine the colours, twist the clay chipolatas into one large sausage, fold in half, twist and roll into a ball, then repeat.

3 Using a rolling pin, roll out your ball to a thickness of 5mm–1cm. The colours should blend beautifully together to create a unique pattern. Place a layer of clingfilm over your clay if it begins to stick to your pin.

4 Draw a 20cm circle onto some tracing paper, using a compass or round object. Place over the rolled-out clay and cut with a craft knife.

5 Pinch off 3 pea-sized pieces from the leftover clay (these will form your tripod base) and wrap the rest in cling film to use in your next kokedama tray.

6 Give the outside of your bowl an oily massage. Place the 3 clay 'peas' in a triangle on top of your upturned bowl. Place your clay circle gently over the bowl and mould a little around the peas and bowl with your fingers. I also like to swirl the bowl around a bit so that the edges of the bowl are a little thinner than the base.

7 Bake the clay according to the packaging directions. Remove from the oven and allow to cool before turning upside down and tapping lightly to loosen your marbled masterpiece. It's lovely to peer inside. You may like the look of your marbled peas from the inside or you may decide to remove them. They quite easily pop out, or you can glue them in to be a permanent fixture.

OPTIONAL

Once the clay is completely cool, you may wish to sand with very fine sandpaper to finish off and tidy the edges. Use a small brush to paint designs on the dish or splatter with metallic paint and allow the paint to dry. Seal the dish with a glaze if you prefer a glossy look.

TIP

Mix individual colours well before rolling, as the basic polymer colours can be too bright for this project. I reference the exquisite tones and combinations of colour in the marbled papers of Ann Muir when considering my palette, but don't worry about matching exactly to a piece of marbled inspiration. The beauty of the task is that you never know how the final stand will turn out and no two will ever look the same. For added opulence, you may like to add flecks of metallic foil to one or two of the colours.

When you are ready and the stand is dry, introduce a kokedama to its new home.
For the sake of domestic harmony, I recommend that you don't place a sodden kokedama
on the stand; all drip-drying should be done over a sink, bath or bowl.

NEVER UNDERESTIMATE THE POWER OF MOSS

NEVER UNDERESTIMATE
THE POWER OF MOSS

MOSS WREATH

—

The beauty of this wreath is that it can be given a different spin throughout the year to coincide with any celebration. Mosses are not bothered about being in soil, as long as the emerald clumps are kept hydrated, a mossy wreath will deck the halls, bejewel any front door or adorn a spring table.

YOU WILL NEED

CUSHION OR BUN MOSS (*LEUCOBRYUM SPP.*)

PAINTBRUSH

FLORAL WIRE

PLIERS

35CM POLYSTYRENE WREATH
(Purchase or customise my shaping one yourself)

OPTIONAL
ribbon, painted eggs and/or natural materials like twigs, vines, pine cones, flowers or seed heads

METHOD

1   Using a paintbrush, brush the dirt and bits of pine needles from your bun or cushion moss, then soak before you start; it's easier to work with when it's damp.

2   Bend the floral wire into a U shape. Cut with pliers so that the U is long enough to penetrate the moss and it will anchor well into the polystyrene. Make many pins, you will need a few to secure each clump.

3   Cup the moss in your hand and firmly hold down on the wreath. Try to maintain its intrinsic moundiness, without flattening. Push the U pins through the moss and into the wreath. Pin around the edges of the clump, until the moss is secure. Continue adding clumps until the wreath is completely covered.

4   Now accessorise your wreath with embellishments.

CARE

LIGHT
Keep your wreath out of direct sunlight, to stop it fading.

WATER
Mist your wreath daily. Mosses are fans of damp environments.

〉

MARKETS

Local markets are great places to source supplies for these projects and most florists can order specific plants on request. These are my favourite markets

NEW COVENT GARDEN FLOWER MARKET

www.newcoventgardenmarket.com/flowers
For buying plants in bulk, bun moss, sheet moss, glass vessels, bamboo sticks

OLD SPITALFIELDS ANTIQUE MARKET

www.oldspitalfieldsmarket.com
The Thursday antique market is great for interesting glassware, crystals and objects to include in your terrarium.

ALYSON MOWAT STUDIO

www.alysonmowat.com
Can source supplies and make bespoke kits for any project you would like to try.

HOBBYCRAFT

www.hobbycraft.co.uk
You can find a range of polystyrene wreaths here.

LEYLAND SDM

https://leylandsdm.co.uk
Stocks general hardware.

N1 GARDEN CENTRE

http://n1gardencentre.co.uk
For specific soil, terrarium plants, carnivorous plants and some water plants.

TESCO

www.tesco.com
The Tesco Low Dust Cat Litter is a purse-friendly alternative to akadama soil.

TRIFFID NURSERIES

www.triffidnurseries.co.uk
Online shop selling carnivorous plants and soil mixes.

WHOLESALE TROPICALS

220 Bethnal Green Road
Bethnal Green London E2 0AA
Source of aquatic terrarium supplies.

ACKNOWLEDGEMENTS

—

I'd like to thank Cath Gratwicke for her lovely
photography; Christopher Moon for his beautiful
illustrations; Evi O for her stylish design; Nadine Tubbs
for her great props; Jason Irving for his helpful edits,
Helena Caldon for her grammar skills; and Claire,
Judith and Kyle for making it all happen.